Beluga Whales

▲ Tammy Kennington

Published in the United States of America by Cherry Lake Publishing
Ann Arbor, Michigan
www.cherrylakepublishing.com

Consultants: Dominique A. Didier, PhD, Associate Professor, Department of Biology, Millersville University;
Marla Conn, ReadAbility, Inc.
Book design and illustration: Sleeping Bear Press

Photo Credits: ©Luna Vandoorne/Shutterstock Images, cover, 1, 29; ©Steve Snodgrass/http://www.flickr.com/
CC-BY-2.0, 5; ©Christopher Meder/Shutterstock Images, 6, 17, 21; ©nailzchap/iStockphoto, 9; ©Dorling Kindersley RF/
Thinkstock, 11; ©J. Helgason/Shutterstock Images, 12; ©Miles Away Photography/Shutterstock Images, 15; ©Hemera/
Thinkstock, 18; ©glen gaffney/Shutterstock Images, 23; ©Anette Holmberg/Shutterstock Images, 25; ©Ivan Histand/
Shutterstock Images, 27

Library of Congress Cataloging-in-Publication Data

Kennington, Tammy, author.
Beluga whales / Tammy Kennington.
    pages cm. — (Exploring our oceans)
  Summary: "Discover facts about beluga whales, including physical features, habitat, life cycle, food,
and threats to these ocean creatures. Photos, captions, and keywords supplement the narrative of this
informational text"— Provided by publisher.
  Audience: 8-12.
  Audience: Grades 4 to 6.
  Includes bibliographical references and index.
  ISBN 978-1-62431-603-6 (hardcover) — ISBN 978-1-62431-615-9 (pbk) —
  ISBN 978-1-62431-627-2 (pdf) — ISBN 978-1-62431-639-5 (ebook)
  1. White whale—Juvenile literature. I. Title.

  QL737.C433K46 2014
  599.5'42—dc23   2013041378

Cherry Lake Publishing would like to acknowledge the work of
The Partnership for 21st Century Skills. Please visit www.p21.org
for more information.

Printed in the United States of America
Corporate Graphics Inc.
January 2014

ABOUT THE AUTHOR

Tammy Kennington holds a bachelor's degree in elementary education and has earned certification
as a reading intervention specialist. She currently serves as a preschool director and tutors children
with dyslexia and related reading disorders. Tammy lives in Colorado Springs, Colorado, with her
husband and four children.

TABLE OF CONTENTS

CHAPTER 1

THE SEA CANARY

What toothed animal has no voice box but earned the nickname sea canary because of the beautiful music it makes? The beluga whale! Scientists believe the sea canary sends messages with at least 11 different sounds. These include mooing, chirping, whistling, and even making a sound like a bell. Its songs can be heard above and below the ocean. These sounds are used to communicate with other whales.

The name beluga comes from the Russian word *bielo*, which means "white." The name is appropriate because

This beluga whale could be communicating with other whales.

unlike other whales, beluga whales are very pale in color. They actually look white.

The beluga whale is small and has a trait unlike other whales. Its seven backbones are not **fused** together. That means this whale can move its neck from side to side. Scientists think this special ability helps the beluga see and capture its prey more easily than other whales. This ocean creature has another unique trait: It can even smile and frown!

Do you notice things about this whale that make you think of other ocean creatures?

LOOK AGAIN

LOOK CLOSELY AT THIS PHOTOGRAPH. HOW ARE BELUGA WHALES SIMILAR TO AND DIFFERENT FROM OTHER WHALES YOU HAVE SEEN?

The beluga whale lives only in the **Northern Hemisphere** and prefers the shallow waters of the Arctic and **subarctic**. A visit to the coasts of Alaska, Canada, Greenland, or Russia might provide you with a glimpse of these gentle animals. A population of beluga whales also lives in the St. Lawrence River in Canada. Many beluga whales stay in the same area all year. But the Arctic belugas migrate south in large herds when the ocean waters freeze.

Beluga whales are social animals and travel in **pods**. Pods can be as small as five whales or as large as 500. Belugas aren't choosy about staying in one pod. Sometimes, beluga whales will move from one pod to another or swim with their closest relative, the narwhal.

With many interesting features, the beluga is an animal worth investigating.

CHAPTER 2

FLIPPERS, FLUKES, AND FUNNY FOREHEADS

Beluga whale fossils have been discovered off the coast of Mexico. Now extinct, these ancestral belugas only lived in mild and tropical climates. As the world's ocean system changed, beluga whales adapted to the colder environment.

The modern beluga whale is specially adapted to living in a cold, icy **habitat**. Its body is shaped at both ends like a submarine, and it has a thick layer of **blubber** that keeps it warm and stores energy. Most whales have a layer of blubber that is about 4 inches

(10.1 cm) thick. But this white whale's fat layer can be as thick as 10.5 inches (26.7 cm). Blubber makes up almost half of the beluga whale's weight!

This cold, icy habitat is perfect for beluga whales.

At birth, baby belugas may be dark gray or brownish gray. As they mature, the calves, or newborns, slowly lose the **pigment** in their skin. By the time a beluga whale reaches maturity, it is a creamy white color with some darker colors on its short, wide flippers and **flukes**. Scientists believe these colors **camouflage** the whales in their snowy surroundings.

What are flippers and flukes? Flippers are the front limbs on either side of the whale's body. From the outside they look like broad paddles. Inside these limbs are a lot like human hands. There are five digits, which look like fingers. **Cartilage** rests between the bones and protects the digits, and the entire limb is covered by skin. The whale uses its flippers to steer.

THINK ABOUT IT

COMPARE AND CONTRAST THE SKELETAL STRUCTURE OF A HUMAN HAND WITH THAT OF A BELUGA WHALE FLIPPER. HOW DO YOU IMAGINE WAYS THEY ARE DIFFERENT AND WAYS THEY ARE THE SAME?

BODY DIAGRAM

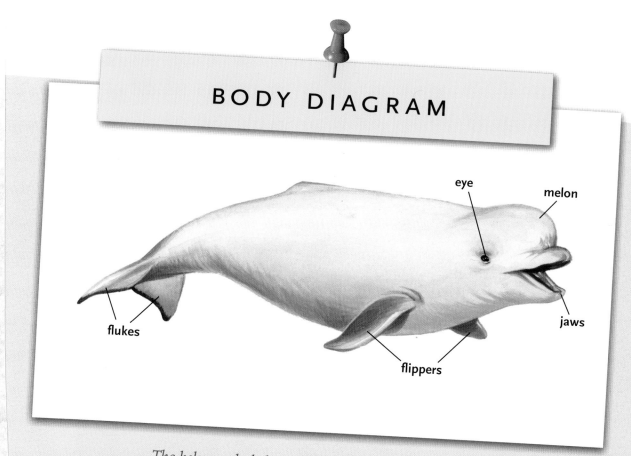

eye

melon

jaws

flukes

flippers

The beluga whale has more blubber than most whales.

The beluga whale has two flukes, or tail sections. They move up and down and help a whale stop when it is swimming. Flukes are covered by heavy tissue and do not contain bones. An adult beluga whale has flukes that are curved along the edges and separated by a deep groove.

The beluga's flukes help it swim.

The beluga's skin is 10 times thicker than a dolphin's and 100 times thicker than that of land mammals. The skin provides protection from freezing water. When the adult's skin turns yellow, it is close to **molting** season. Unique among its closest relatives, the beluga whale sheds old skin every July. It rubs against gravel or sand until the new, white layer of skin is uncovered.

The beluga whale also has a different kind of head than other whales. Its forehead, or melon, looks swollen and rounded. Made up of fats, it sits in front of the **blowhole** and hangs over the nose. The melon changes shape when the whale makes sounds. Many scientists believe the melon is used to produce these sounds.

The beluga whale has highly developed senses, too. Able to hear as well beneath the water as above it, the beluga detects noise through its jaw. Sound waves travel through the fat-filled lower jaw to the middle and inner ears. Then the sound waves are sent to the listening center in the brain.

The beluga uses a special process called **echolocation** to learn about its environment. Echolocation is a trait shared by a few other marine mammals and also bats. The beluga makes a series of clicking sounds, which bounce off of objects in the habitat. The clicks return as echoes and pass through the jaw. The echoes provide information about prey, holes in the ice, and more.

Sleep is important for all animals, but the beluga has an unusual approach to getting its rest. Instead of closing its eyes and lying down, one side of the beluga's brain falls asleep. The other side of the brain stays awake. This allows the beluga to swim, look for predators, and watch over its young. When one side of the brain has rested, the other side has a turn.

A small whale, the average male beluga is between 14 and 16 feet (4.3 and 4.9 m) long and weighs close to 3,300 pounds (1,497 kg). A female beluga measures from 13 to 14 feet (4 to 4.3 m) long and weighs about 3,000 pounds

(1,361 kg). Both males and females are as heavy as a compact car.

Even though the beluga is much smaller than most other whales, its remarkable traits seem to make it larger than life. ◢

The beluga whale is not as large as most other whales.

CHAPTER 3

Hunting and Eating

The beluga whale has a healthy appetite. It eats 40 to 50 pounds (18 to 22.7 kg) of food every day. Its meal choices include about 100 different kinds of sea creatures that it can find easily. Some favorites are octopus, squid, sandworms, and small fish like cod and flounder.

Beluga whales hunt in both the open ocean waters and coastal areas. Females and their calves often choose calm, shallow areas for hunting. Mixed pods of males and females without calves prefer colder, deeper waters.

Alaskan belugas have traveled as far as 430 miles (692 km) across the open ocean. They even go to areas that are 90 percent covered by sea ice and will hunt for miles beneath the ice!

This group is hunting for food in shallow waters of the ocean.

Beluga whales often hunt alone. However, they also will hunt in small groups of five or more to herd schools of fish toward shallower water. The beluga usually goes no more than 20 to 100 feet (6.1 to 30.5 m) beneath the water's surface. But it has been known to dive as deep as 2,123 feet (647 m) and remain underwater for up to 20 minutes when hunting.

Beluga whales have few predators.

The beluga whale has flexible lips, which are a useful hunting tool. The lips create a stream of air that dislodges animals from the seafloor. Then the whale uses a sucking motion to pull in the prey. Although the beluga has 40 teeth by the time it is an adult, it cannot chew its prey. The beluga usually tears apart larger prey, but it swallows smaller prey whole.

GO DEEPER

REVIEW THIS PARAGRAPH ABOUT THE BELUGA WHALE'S HUNTING TECHNIQUE. DO YOU KNOW OF ANOTHER ANIMAL THAT SWALLOWS ITS PREY WHOLE?

The beluga whale is at the top of the food chain and considered an **apex** predator. While the beluga feasts on many types of food, this little whale's only natural predators are killer whales and polar bears.

CHAPTER 4

LIFE AS A BELUGA

When the beluga whale is between seven and nine years old, it is mature enough to mate. The female breeds in the late winter or spring. She forms a pod with other beluga mothers and gives birth to her calf. Rarely, belugas may have twins. Females have babies only about every three years. This slow birthrate affects some of the threatened beluga whale populations.

A female beluga is pregnant for 14 or 15 months before her calf is born live. A beluga calf begins life as a baby that is 5 feet (1.5 m) long and 119 to 140 pounds (54-to-63.5 kg)!

Born either headfirst or tail first, the calf can swim right away. The mother and a young female whale guide the newborn to the water's surface. There, the calf takes its first breath. Like all mammals, beluga whales breathe air,

A mother beluga will help her baby get to the water's surface for air.

so it's important that the calf breathe right away or it could drown. The calf is usually born between May and July. Mothers have their babies in bays where the water is warmer. Newborns have not yet developed the blubber they need to protect them from cold waters.

Like other mammals, mother belugas nurse their calves. The calf depends on its mother for all of its food for the first year of life. Once it has teeth, the calf supplements its diet with small fish and shrimp. The young whale relies on its mother's rich milk until it is close to two years old. During this time, the baby beluga mimics its mother's behavior. By the time the calf is weaned, it has learned how to survive on its own.

Scientists can estimate the age of a beluga by studying its teeth. A beluga whale develops layers on its teeth as it ages. By studying a section of a tooth, researchers can guess at the whale's age. Most experts agree that beluga whales can live to be at least 35 years old in their natural habitat.

Mother beluga's help their babies learn skills needed to survive.

LOOK AGAIN

Look closely at this photograph. What physical characteristics do you notice that would help a baby beluga whale swim to the water's surface at birth?

CHAPTER 5

LET THE BELUGA SING!

After careful study, scientists believe that belugas living in the wild and belugas in human care have the same life expectancy. The beluga's life span in the wild is 35 to 50 years. The oldest belugas in captivity are more than 40 years old.

Polar bears and killer whales hunt beluga whales, but are not a threat to their survival. The belugas are at risk from many other hazards. One natural danger is when beluga whales get trapped under ice. Whales can suffocate or starve if they cannot find a route to the water's surface for air. Entire pods sometimes die as a result.

For hundreds of years, beluga whales have been harvested for their meat, blubber, and skin. During the 1800s and 1900s, fishing for belugas was a booming

Beluga whales can become prey for polar bears.

business. Europeans and Americans used blubber and fat from the melon to make soap, margarine, and oil for lighthouses. The skin was used to make shoes and shoelaces. In 1911 whalers killed more than 20,000 beluga whales in the Arctic Ocean. From 1994 to 1998, beluga whales in Cook Inlet, Alaska, were hunted and killed in large numbers. The Cook Inlet whale population has not recovered yet.

Around the world, most beluga populations are steady. But populations in some areas have been listed as Near-threatened by the International Union for Conservation of Nature. This means belugas are close to or are likely to become threatened in the future.

Pollution is a serious danger for beluga whales. Researchers believe high levels of chemicals have leaked into the water from metal factories along the St. Lawrence River. These chemicals, called PHAs, are known to cause cancer in humans. One in four belugas living in this region has cancer. Scientists do not have any proof, but they suspect the sea canary swallows toxic dirt when it scoops prey into its mouth and develops cancer as a result.

Water pollution is a threat to beluga whales.

Increased ocean noise is also a possible threat to the beluga whale. Underwater noise from ocean vessels, ferryboat traffic, and oil drilling might make it difficult for the beluga to communicate or use echolocation. Without these skills, the beluga will not be able to locate prey or escape from predators.

In 2013, there were more than 150,000 beluga whales worldwide. If scientists, conservation groups, businesses, and other people work together, the beluga should be swimming the ocean for hundreds of years to come. It is important to keep the song of the sea canary alive.

This beluga whale is cared for in an aquarium.

LOOK AGAIN

LOOK AT THIS BELUGA WHALE LIVING IN CAPTIVITY. DO YOU BELIEVE BELUGAS SHOULD BE CARED FOR AT AQUARIUMS FOR RESEARCH, CONSERVATION, AND EDUCATION? WHY OR WHY NOT?

THINK ABOUT IT

- Write three questions about beluga whales. Discuss them with a partner or small group.

- Read chapter 2 again. Describe three important beluga whale adaptations. What do you think is the most interesting adaptation? What else would you like to know?

- What are some threats the beluga whale faces today? Do you think it is important to protect the belugas? Why or why not?

- Visit the library and check out another book about beluga whales. How does the information in that book compare to the information in this one?

LEARN MORE

FURTHER READING

Gouck, Maura. *Whales*. Chicago: Child's World, 1991.

Landau, Elaine. *Beluga Whales*. Berkeley Heights, NJ: Enslow, 2010.

Nicklin, Flip, and Linda Nicklin. *Face to Face with Whales*. Washington, DC: National Geographic Children's Books, 2010.

WEB SITES

National Geographic—Lifestyles of Beluga Whales
http://video.nationalgeographic.com/video/animals/mammals-animals/whales/whale_beluga
This video shows stunning images of a beluga whale pod migrating to the Gulf of St. Lawrence.

Sea World—Beluga Whales
www.seaworld.org/animal-info/info-books/beluga/index.htm
Readers can learn more about beluga whales including how they communicate and how they care for their young.

GLOSSARY

apex (AY-peks) at the very top

blowhole (BLOH-hohl) nostril used for breathing air and producing whistling sounds

blubber (BLUHB-er) fat layer found between the skin and muscles of a whale

camouflage (KAM-uh-flahj) an animal's natural coloring that enables it to blend in with its surroundings

cartilage (KAHR-tuh-lij) a tough, flexible animal tissue that is whitish or yellowish in color

conservation (kon-ser-VEY-shuhn) preventing waste or loss

echolocation (eh-koh-loh-KAY-shun) a process for locating a distant object by sound waves reflected back from that object

flukes (FLOOKS) triangular parts of a whale's tail

fused (FYOOZD) blended or united

habitat (HAB-ih-tat) the place where animals or plants naturally live

molting (MOHLT-eng) losing old skin, feathers, or fur so that new ones can grow

Northern Hemisphere (NOR-thurn HEM-uhs-feer) the half of the earth that is between the North Pole and the equator

pigment (PIG-muhnt) substance that gives plants or animals their color

pods (PODZ) groups of whales or dolphins

subarctic (suhb-AHRK-tik) regions directly outside of the arctic circle

INDEX

[21ST CENTURY SKILLS LIBRARY]